Pet Cents

by Margaret Fetty

STECK-VAUGHN
Harcourt Supplemental Publishers

www.steck-vaughn.com

Contents

Pet Cents

Pets are fun to watch and play with, but they also need food, water, and care. It takes time to care for a pet. It also takes money to buy a pet and all of the things you will need to take care of it.

Different pets cost different amounts of money. You will need to save your money to buy the pet you want. Some children save their money in piggy banks or jars.

penny = 1¢   nickel = 5¢

dime = 10¢   quarter = 25¢

one dollar = $1.00

Is this enough money to buy a pet? To find out, you will need to count the money. Start by putting the bills and coins into groups. Next, add the bills and coins that are worth the most. Then add the rest of the coins as you go.

$1.00 $1.25 $1.50 $1.60 $1.65 $1.70 $1.71

7

Goldfish

Goldfish
50¢

If you do not have much room for a pet, then a goldfish might be the perfect pet for you. Most goldfish are bright orange. They have long fins and tails. Pet goldfish can live in special bowls or tanks.

If a goldfish costs 50¢, is this enough money to buy a pet goldfish?

If a goldfish costs 50¢, this is enough money to buy this pet. There will even be 3¢ left over.

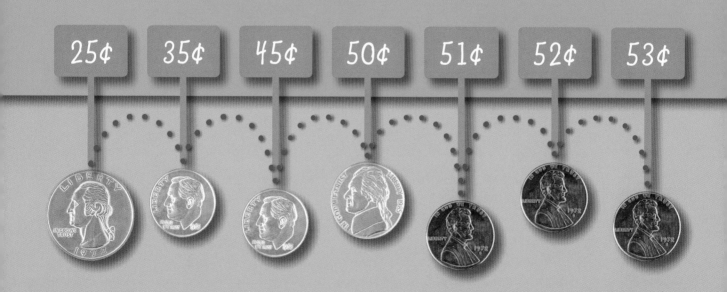

| 25¢ | 35¢ | 45¢ | 50¢ | 51¢ | 52¢ | 53¢ |

If you decide to buy a goldfish, you will need to keep its home clean all the time. Feed it just a pinch of fish food every day. If you can do all this, then a goldfish might be the perfect pet for you.

Turtles

Turtles
92¢

If you have a little more space, then a turtle might be the perfect pet for you. Turtles are usually green. They swim in water and walk around on land. Glass tanks make good homes for pet turtles.

If a turtle costs 92¢, is this enough money to buy a pet turtle?

If a turtle costs 92¢, this is exactly enough money to buy this pet. There will not be any money left over.

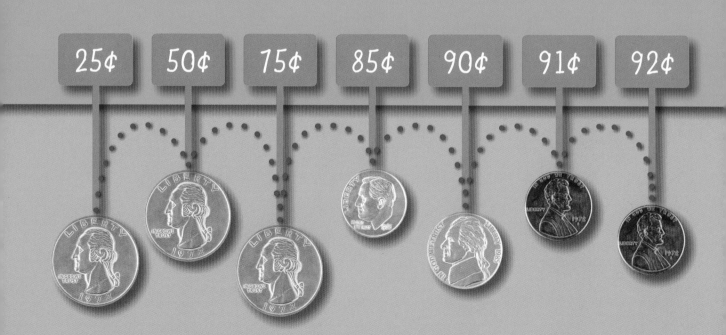

25¢ 50¢ 75¢ 85¢ 90¢ 91¢ 92¢

If you decide to buy a turtle, you will need to give it a good home with clean water for swimming, a rock for climbing, and a light for sunning. You will need to feed your turtle special turtle food. If you can do all this, then a turtle might be the perfect pet for you.

Hamsters

Hamsters $1.30

If you would like a furry pet, then a hamster might be the perfect pet for you. Hamsters have soft fur and like to be held gently. They do not make very much noise. Pet hamsters can live in tanks or cages.

If a hamster costs $1.30, is this enough money to buy a pet hamster?

If a hamster costs $1.30, this is enough money to buy this pet. There will even be 1¢ left over.

25¢ 50¢ 75¢ $1.00 $1.25 $1.30 $1.31

If you decide to buy a hamster, it will need many things. It will need a tank or cage with a food dish, a water bottle, and an exercise wheel. Hamsters need to be handled very gently. If you can do all this, then a hamster might be the perfect pet for you.

Parakeets

Parakeets
$2.00

If you would like a pet that can chirp, then a parakeet might be the perfect pet for you. Parakeets are small birds that are usually green or blue. They can learn to talk if people teach them. Pet parakeets live in cages.

If a parakeet costs $2.00, is this enough money to buy a pet parakeet?

If a parakeet costs $2.00, this is not quite enough money to buy this pet. You would need 10¢ more to buy the parakeet.

$1.00 $1.25 $1.50 $1.75 $1.85 $1.90

If you decide to buy a parakeet, it will need a large cage with food, water, and special bird toys. Parakeets need attention and care, so you will need to spend time with your pet every day. If you can do all this, then a parakeet might be the perfect pet for you.

Saving for the Perfect Pet

Saving money to buy a pet can be fun! For each coin you save, learn one new thing about your pet. In time, you can buy your perfect pet and give it a great home.

24